Uranus
The Ice Planet

By Greg Roza

Gareth Stevens
Publishing

Please visit our Web site, www.garethstevens.com. For a free color catalog of all our high-quality books, call toll free 1-800-542-2595 or fax 1-877-542-2596.

Library of Congress Cataloging-in-Publication Data

Roza, Greg.
 Uranus : the ice planet / Greg Roza.
   p. cm. — (Our solar system)
 Includes index.
 ISBN 978-1-4339-3843-6 (pbk.)
 ISBN 978-1-4339-3844-3 (6-pack)
 ISBN 978-1-4339-3842-9 (lib. bdg.)
 1. Uranus (Planet)—Juvenile literature. I. Title.
 QB681.R69 2011
 523.47—dc22

                                    2010006041

First Edition

Published in 2011 by
Gareth Stevens Publishing
111 East 14th Street, Suite 349
New York, NY 10003

Designer: Christopher Logan
Editor: Greg Roza

Photo credits: Cover, back cover, pp. 1, 7 (Uranus), 19 courtesy NASA/JPL; pp. 5, 11, 17 Shutterstock.com; pp. 7 (Earth), 13 (Earth) courtesy NASA/MODIS/USGS; p. 13 (Uranus) courtesy NASA/JPL/STScI; p. 15 Time Life Pictures/Getty Images; p. 21 courtesy NASA/JPL/USGS.

Printed in the United States of America

CPSIA compliance information: Batch #CS10GS: For further information contact Gareth Stevens, New York, New York at 1-800-542-2595.

Contents

Boldface words appear in the glossary.

Meet the Ice Planet

Uranus is the seventh planet from the sun in our **solar system**. Since it is so far away from the sun, it is very cold and icy.

Our Solar System

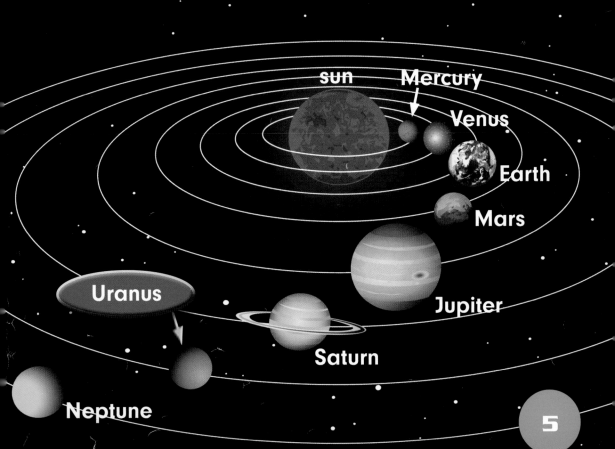

sun

Mercury

Venus

Earth

Mars

Jupiter

Uranus

Saturn

Neptune

Uranus is the third-largest planet in the solar system. It is about four times as wide as Earth.

Moving All the Time

Uranus **orbits** the sun, just like the other planets do. Since it is so far away, Uranus takes a little more than 84 years to orbit the sun!

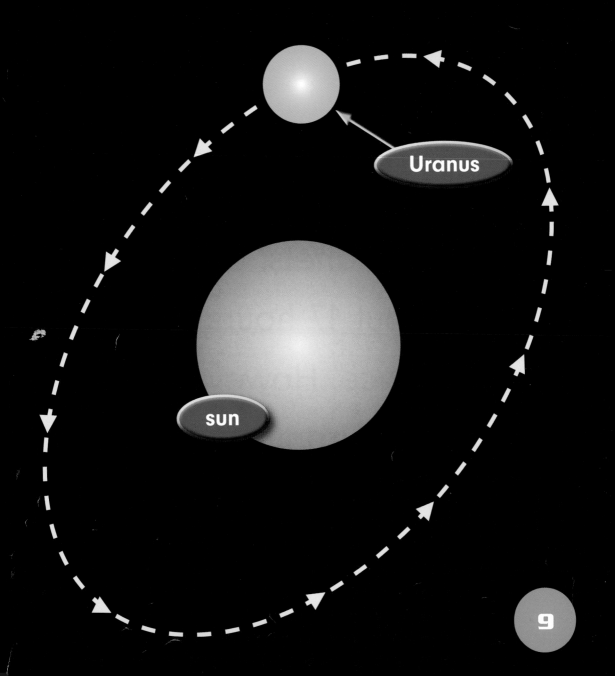

Uranus

sun

Uranus spins around, just like the other planets. Uranus takes about 17 hours to spin around once. However, the air around Uranus spins much faster than that.

Uranus spins on its side! Scientists think another planet may have crashed into Uranus long ago. The crash might have tipped Uranus on its side.

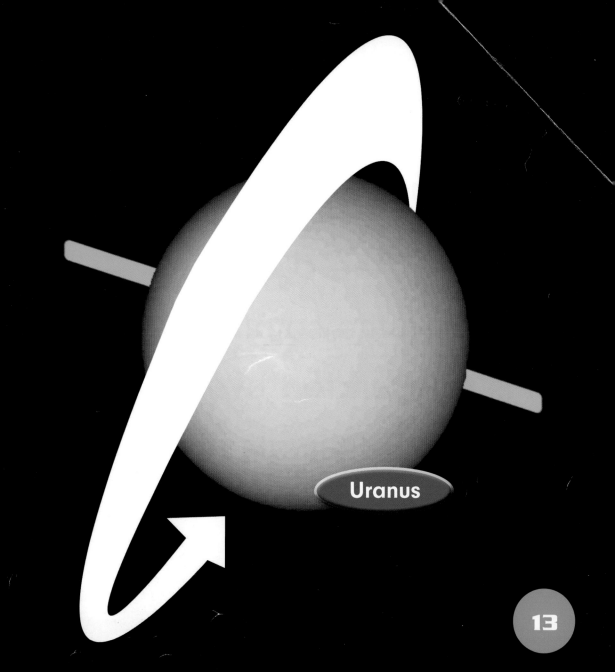

Uranus

Icy Clouds

Uranus is the coldest planet in the solar system. It is **surrounded** by icy clouds. Uranus also has rings like Saturn does.

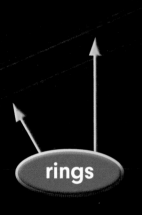

rings

15

Uranus looks completely blue. This is because of a gas around Uranus called **methane**.

Beneath the Clouds

Scientists think that Uranus might have a huge ocean beneath its icy clouds. They also think the center of the planet is rocky.

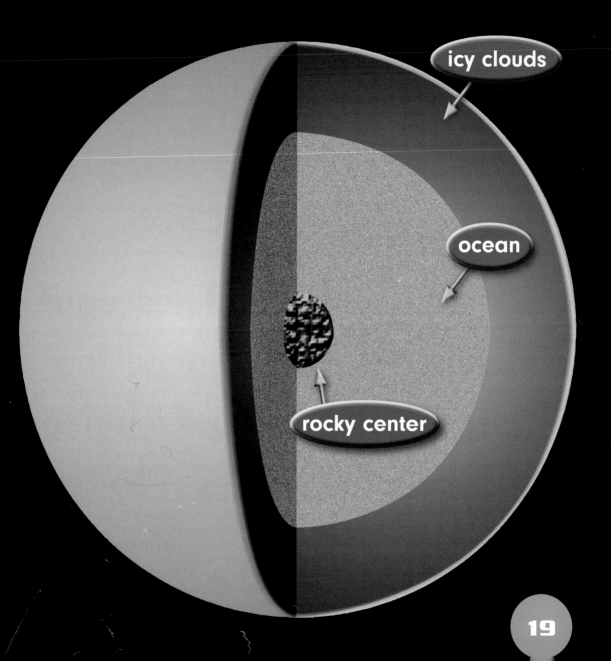

icy clouds

ocean

rocky center

The Ice Planet Up Close

Scientists have used **telescopes** and **probes** to learn about the "Ice Planet." They have learned that Uranus has at least 27 moons

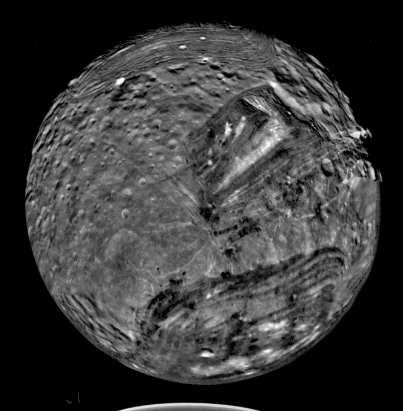

moon of Uranus

Glossary

methane: a common gas in the solar system. On Earth, it is found in natural gas.

orbit: to travel in a circle or oval around something

probe: an unmanned spaceship

solar system: the sun and all the space objects that orbit it, including the planets and their moons

surround: to circle

telescope: a tool that makes faraway objects look larger and nearer

For More Information

Books

Howard, Fran. *Uranus*. Edina, MN: ABDO Publishing, 2008.

Vogt, Gregory L. *Uranus*. Minneapolis, MN: Lerner Publications, 2010.

Web Sites

Uranus

www.kidsastronomy.com/uranus.htm
Learn about Uranus with the help of diagrams and links to more information about the solar system.

Uranus: The Sideways Planet

solarsystem.nasa.gov/planets/profile.cfm?Object=Uranus&Display=Kids
Explore this NASA Web site about Uranus with links to more information about the solar system.

Index

About the Author

Greg Roza has written and edited educational materials for young readers for the past ten years. He has a master's degree in English from the State University of New York at Fredonia. Roza has long had an interest in scientific topics and spends much of his spare time reading about the cosmos.